산소의

색을

볼 수

있다면

If We Could See

the Color of

Oxygen

산소의 색을 볼 수 있다면

2021년 1월 15일 초판 1쇄 발행
2021년 1월 15일 초판 1쇄 인쇄

지은이 | 김유나

인쇄 | 아레스트 (s-lin@hanmail.net)
표지 | theambitious factory

펴낸이 | 이장우
펴낸곳 | 꿈공장 플러스
출판등록 | 제 406-2017-000160호
주소 | 서울시 성북구 보국문로 꿈공장 1층
전화 | 010-4679-2734
팩스 | 031-624-4527
이메일 | ceo@dreambooks.kr
홈페이지 | www.dreambooks.kr
인스타그램 | @dreambooks.ceo

ISBN | 979-11-89129-78-1

정 가 | 12,000원

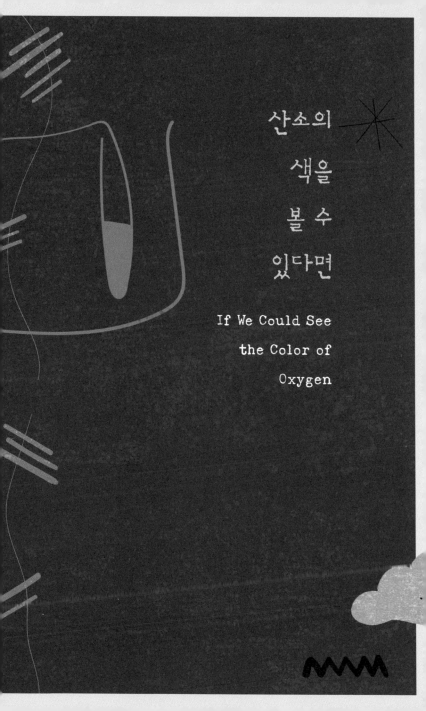

산소의
색을
볼 수
있다면

If We Could See
the Color of
Oxygen

네 번째 색. 이별과 상실

다섯 번째 색. 다시 자연으로

Everyone has the depths of the soul and there exist
many layers of emotions. Sometimes, the serene surface
of the water and its depth where you cannot breathe
coexist or contrast each other, but what matters is that
all layers of emotions have their meanings. As much as
love and joy do, loss and anguish send us signals that
tell us in what state our minds are. Thus, at times,
we need to look at those emotions neutrally, without
judgment. Even in difficult and hurtful times, there can
be found happiness and beauty.

I've long been thinking, wanting, and trying to write
a bilingual book. I wanted this book to contain both
the rhyme in English poems and the conciseness in
Korean poems. Most of all, I wanted to accentuate how

it is rare for one language to surpass another by its superiority. I hope you would blissfully experience the similarities and differences in sets of bilingual poems.

Lastly, I meditated a lot especially while writing this book. Some poems were written as if they were meditations themselves. It can be an arduous process to introspect and excavate the true colors of your emotions. That is part of reason I want to share my experience and communicate with you through my poems. As if to reflect yourself on the surface of a deep, beautiful pond, or as if you are one for that reason, I wish that you would go on a journey with me to look inside ourselves to meet our candid emotions.

모든 사람은 마음의 깊이를 지니고 있고 우리의 감정은 여러 단계로 이루어져 있습니다. 때론 잔잔한 수면의 가벼움과 숨 쉴 수 없도록 깊은 해저의 무거움이 공존하기도, 서로를 대조하기도 합니다. 공통점은, 모든 마음의 깊이가 의미 있다는 것입니다. 사랑과 기쁨 못지않게 상실과 고통의 감정들도 부정적이기만 하지는 않습니다. 그 또한 마음이 우리에게 보내는, 우리의 상태를 알려주는, 중요한 신호이기에 우리는 때로 그와 같은 감정들을 중립적으로, 판단 없이, 바라볼 필요가 있습니다. 아픔과 어려움 속에도 행복과 아름다움은 존재할 수 있습니다.

2개국어로 책을 쓰는 일은 오랫동안 생각하고, 바라고, 시도해 온 일입니다. 영시의 라임과 한시의 함축성을 동시에 이 시집에 담고 싶기도 했습니다. 무엇보다, 한 언어가 다른 언어에 비해 우월한 경우가 드물다는 것을 나타내고 싶었습니다. 읽는 분께서 한 쌍의 2개국어 시 안에서 같음과 다름을 즐겁게 경험하시기를 바랍니다.

  마지막으로, 이 책을 쓰면서 특히 명상을 많이 했고, 또, 명상하는 마음으로 쓴 시도 많습니다. 나의 감정들을 성찰하고 있는 그대로의 색채를 발굴하는 일은 때로 무척 어려운 일입니다. 그래서 더욱 그러한 경험을, 읽는 분과 소통하듯 나누고 싶었습니다. 깊고 아름다운 연못에 자신을 비추어 보듯, 또 자신이 그런 연못이 되어 보듯, 저와 함께 솔직한 감정을 들여다보는 내면 여행을 떠나 주시지 않겠습니까?

World

Angry ranting over
Wine decanting

Lovers panting under
Willows slanting

Priests chanting on
Creations enchanting.

세계

무르익는 술잔 위
오고 가는 언쟁들

비스듬한 버드나무 아래
거친 숨을 쉬는 연인들

매혹적인 피조물에 관해
설교하는 성직자.

First Color --

Meditation and Mind-love

As trivial and as great as oxygen…

We do not judge anything that occurs today.

명상과 마음 사랑

사소하고 경이롭게 산소같이…

오늘 일어나는 어떤 일도 판단하지 않습니다.

Margin of You

While staring at a tree,
Have you looked at the space
Between the branches?

While lying down on a bed,
Have you felt the margin
Of your body?

Rather than the wind touching your skin,
Have you beamed for a petal
Shaken by the wind?

While he sings,
Have you listened to his breath
In-between the lyrics?

While she speaks,
Have you pondered upon the meanings
Of her hesitation?

When you look at the light between
The branches and not the tree
Itself,

You are a light enough being
That is finally bearable,
A rest.

나의 여백

나무를 바라볼 때
가지 사이의 공간에
초점을 맞춰 본 적이 있는가

침대에 누웠을 때
내 몸의 여백을
느껴 본 적이 있는가

살에 닿는 바람보다
바람에 흔들리는 꽃의
그림자로 인해 웃은 적이 있는가

그가 노래할 때
가사와 가사 사이의 숨결에
귀를 기울여 보았는가

그녀가 말할 때
문장과 문장 사이의 머뭇거림을
헤아려 보았는가

나무를 보지 않고
가지 사이로 드는 빛을
쳐다보면

비로소 참을 수 있을 만큼 가벼운 존재,
쉼.

The Strength of the Fragile

Like the impression I saw in your fragile veins
That contained all the warmth and livelihood of
the world,
Though small, the undeniable red palpitated
In the absence of emotions of light or dark

The strange tone of blue at 7:40 a.m.
Is dying my mind in a deep grey hue
In its afterimage of a morning
Which shall linger.

어린 것들의 강함

너의 신체 중 가녀린 실핏줄에서
세상 모든 온기와 생명력을 보았던 인상,
작지만 부인할 수는 없던
그 새빨간 두근거림처럼

빛과 어둠 속 감정의 부재보다 7시 40분의
묘하게 푸른 색조가 마음을 옅고 깊은
회색빛으로 물들이는 어느 아침의
기억에 남을, 잔상.

Spring Dream

The atmosphere out
Is couple degrees warmer
Than my inside

All elements are subtly elevated
In their moods
Without an exaggeration

I breathe in sublime grace
With winter's freshness
Still lingering

Then I fall in a dream
Of pink and faded orange.

봄의 꿈

기온은 마음의 체온보다 몇도 높고
모든 원소는 미묘하게 고조되어
나는 전혀 격양됨 없는 숨을 쉬네

우아한 봄의 공기엔
아직 겨울의 상쾌함이 머물러,

나는 이만 지련다—
핑크와 빛바랜 오렌지 색 꿈으로.

Timeless Nights
(Insomnia)

On some nights time is long enough
For people to build a civilization
That would break down the great walls
Into a ruin

On those nights there is an ample time
For a camelia to bloom
In its full language
And without a hint of remorse
In its usage of cliched expressions

But on those nights,
Poets are forbidden
To use any death-related metaphors

Even though people would see
Their lives fleet
In permanent lights beneath
Their flickering eyelids
All night long.

시간만이 존재하는 밤
(불면)

어떤 밤은 누군가 문명을 짓고는
장성을 무너뜨려
폐허로 만들 만큼
충분히 길다

그런 밤엔
동백꽃이 온갖 언어로 피어나고도
낡은 표현을 자책하지 않을 만큼
시간이 많다

하지만 그런 밤엔,
시인은 죽음과 관련된 은유를
쓰지 않았으며,

그럼에도 모두가
밤새도록, 밤이 새도록,
깜빡이는 것들을 보곤 했다.

Dear Rose

Thorn,

Do not lose your might,

For many raindrops fell

To let a beauty like you

Bloom.

장미에게

가시야,
울지 마라

너란 꽃을
피우려고

비가
많이 왔다,

내리는구나.

Night Rescue of a Traumatized Child in the Sad yet Serene Condolences

"Strong baby, light is lit all night,

So, there is no need to fret,

Much less to apologize."

I see her precious hands folded

In rigid politeness on her small knees

And gently free them with my grown-up hands

Once covering them fully with warmth.

"You are all right, now, I am not leaving you,"

"There, there, sleep tight, my child-hood,

Sweet dreams and remember that you are loved."

트라우마가 있는 아이를 구조하는
슬프고 고요한 밤

"강한 아가야, 불은 밤새 켜져 있을 거란다.
무서워할 필요 없고,
사과할 필요는 더더욱 없단다."
소녀의 두 손은 곱고 예의 바르게 포개진 채
무릎 위에 놓여 있다.
나는 소녀의 손을 나의 어른 손바닥으로
따스하게 한 번 감싼 뒤 자유롭게 풀어 준다.
"넌 이제 괜찮아, 내가 널 떠나지 않을 거야,
자, 자, 잘 자렴, 나의 어린, 시절아,
좋은 꿈 꾸고 네가 사랑받고 있다는 걸 기억하거라."

No Time Endured is Futile

No time endured is futile
For All heavy branches
Will bear their fruits

Truths that set you free
Are not excavated by digging the earth,
Or under a scrutiny on microscopes,

But rather, they tend to
ripen in time

Those who wait will meet
A day on which all see
The truths that make sense

And the greatest thing
I will ever learn about you
Is what time has allowed
For me to know.

견뎌 낸 시간 중 하찮은 시간은 없다

모든 가지는
열매를 견딘다

자유케 하는 진실은
땅속에도 현미경 아래에도 없다

시간 안에 익을 뿐

기다리는 자는
통용되는 진실을 본다

내가 그대에 관해 알 수 있는 것은
시간이 나에게 허락한 것 뿐.

Truthful Fantasy

As a child, my reality often blurred into fantasy,
and fantasy, into reality.
As an adult, I wonder how it is any different
except both got very complex
and I am more willing to draw
a clear line between them.

On nights with nightmares,
there is a stream in my fantasy that I visit.
This is a place that nobody else knows, that I like,
Where there are wind, grasses, and water.

It is a magic stream so you never fall in it.

It is a safe place.

Today's tree nearby the stream
Let its leaves fall
Onto the stream without any effort
And it was letting go

The leaves flowed on the stream
and left me,
left the tree,
getting farther and farther

At least tonight,
Nearby this bright stream,
I shall let go
Of my guests that are my thoughts,
Having them on each leaf

As I see them
Get far away from me…
I empty myself.

진솔한 환상

아이였을 때는 판타지와 현실이 서로를 넘나들었다.
어른인 지금, 판타지도 현실도 복잡해지고
내가 둘 사이에 선을 긋고 싶어 할 뿐,
무엇이 그리 다른지.
악몽을 꾸는 밤 내가 찾는 환상 속 냇가가 있다.
이곳은 나만 아는, 내가 좋아하는,
바람과 풀과 물이 있는 곳이다.
절대 빠질 일 없는 마법의 냇가다.

이곳은 안전하다.

오늘 냇가의 나무는
아무 노력 없이
잎을 냇가에 떨궜고,
그것은 보내 줌이었다

잎은 물에 실려,
나로부터,
나무로부터,
멀어져 갔다

오늘 밤 만은
이 밝은 냇가에서
나에게 찾아오는 생각 손님을
나뭇잎 위에 하나씩 실어
보내드린다

나로부터
멀어지는 것을
바라보며…
비워 신나.

Practice

Sometimes, practice

Makes us perfect

And other times,

It allows us to accept

Our imperfection.

연습

연습은,
때론 우리를 완벽하게 만들어 주기도,
때론 완벽할 수 없음을
받아들일 수 있게도,
해 준다.

Second Color --

Love and Joy

Eternity is nothing but
A boring moment

A moment is nothing but
An eternity where there is love

However,
If you and I are together,
We will live an eternal moment.

사랑과 기쁨

영원이 별건가,
지루한 순간이지

찰나가 별건가,
사랑이 있는 영원이지

허나,
너와 내가 함께라면
우리는 영원한 찰나를 살 것이니.

Upon Meeting You if You Would Allow Me

I open the invisible door
Leading into your world
Walking down your corridor
As carefully as possible

If we ever get to your rooms
That are more intimate
I'd let myself sink
In your air that is different

If you would allow me,
May I soak myself
In the tub of water
That is your heart.

당신을 만나 허락하신다면

그대의 세계로 통하는
보이지 않는 문을 열고
조심스레 조심스레
그대의 복도를 걷겠습니다

서재나 침실같이 친밀한 공간에
허락하신다면
당신의 다른 공기에
젖어 보겠습니다

허락하신다면,
당신의 심장 안
욕조에
좀 누워도 되겠습니까.

While Looking at Fingernails

You said I was like a kid
When you saw my small fingernails

My thirty-year-old round fingernails shyly laughed

If the size of my fingernails
was proportionate to my age,
If the size of your feet
was proportionate to your age,
If our ages were proportionate to our ages,
They would be strange phenomena

I became apologetic
When I saw your big fingernails

Your worn out fingerprints underneath
Your fingernails began laughing again

While tracing our lost hours
We grew in our full bodies
Your fingernails were clipped
To fit the degree of your labor

Perhaps,

You might be right
That ages are not proportionate to ages,
As my fingernails turn pink
Without the help of balsam flowers

As our fingernails touch each other
Laughing from time to time
As our cheeks turn pink
When we hold each other's hands.

손톱을 바라보고 있으면

내 작은 손톱을 보다가
너는 내가 아이 같다고 말했다

서른 살도 넘은 동그란 손톱이 빙그르르 웃었다

내 손톱의 크기가 나이에 비례한다면
네 발의 크기가 나이에 비례한다면
우리의 나이가 나이에 비례한다면
그건 조금 이상한 일

네 커다란 손톱을 보다가
나는 손톱의 각질처럼 미안해졌다
손톱 아래 닳은 지문들이 다시 웃는다
사라진 시간들을 더듬으며
온몸으로 우리는 자랐다 네 손톱은
깎였다 필요한 노동의 강도에 알맞게

어쩌면,

네 말이 맞을지도 모르겠다
나이는 나이에 비례하지 않고
나의 손톱은 봉숭아 물 없이도
아직 붉게 물드니 말이다

너와 나의 손톱이 맞닿아
피식피식 웃고 있으니 말이다
두 손 잡고 있으니
볼까지 붉어지는 것을 보니 말이다.

Sururu Today

All our breaths inhaled
Wear the color of ocean waves tickling the sand
And caress our hearts continuously
That we bend our posture a bit to the front

All our breaths exhaled
Wear small laces of the waves
And laugh like girls gathered at a party
That we at last lower our eyes halfway

Today, sururu,
We gladly welcome the joy surging
Today, sururu,
We let go of worries without holding onto them

Sururu,
Today is
Permeating
Into ourselves.

오늘 하루 스르르

들이쉬는 모든 숨이
모래를 간지럽히는 파도의 색을 입고
계속, 계속, 심장을 간지럽혀서
우리는 앞으로 조금 굽은 자세를 한다

내쉬는 모든 숨이
파도의 작은 레이스를 걸치고
파티하는 소녀들의 웃음을 자아내서
우리는 비로소 눈을 반 내리뜬다

오늘 하루 스르르
밀려오는 설렘을 반가이 맞이하고
오늘 하루 스르르
쓸려가는 걱정을 막지 않고 보내 준다

스르르,
오늘 하루가
우리에게
스며들고 있다.

What Remains

I love those that remain
Rather than those unchanging

Like the sun and god,
Or the stories about gods,

Like the inseparable structure of atoms
Or the imperishable nature of energy,

Without forcing, without caging,
Though you might not be unchanging,
I like you for just remaining.

남아 있는

변하지 않는 것 보다
변하더라도 남아 있는 것들을 사랑한다

해처럼, 신처럼, 또는
신에 관한 이야기처럼

원소의 쪼갤 수 없는 구조처럼,
어떤 형태든 불멸하는 에너지처럼

애쓰지 않아도, 붙잡지 않아도,
불변은 아닐지 어도,
남아 있는 네가 좋다.

Pieces of a Night's Dream

Dreams of shimmer
Break into dawn

Pieces that linger
Pierce torpid bone

Glowing once dimmer
Before wearing out.

꿈의 파편

동이 트는 소리에 간밤의 꿈은 바스락,
부서져 새벽녘으로 달아나네

빛이 되어 날지 못한 파편만이
게으른 나의 뼈를 찔러 대며,
사그라 흩어지기 전,

단 한 번 더 반짝, 거려보네.
꿈의 파편이, 별이 지듯,
어제의 조각이.

Sister's Bedroom
Where There is Piano Music

An ashen room

No, not that grey
You just pictured
But lighter and brighter
With a hint of turquoise as

The gravity-defying
Dusts float along the
Music flowing
Out of

Her pale fingers.

피아노 음악이 흐르는
언니의 방

잿빛 방

당신이 방금 상상하신
그 잿빛 말고
더 가볍고 더 밝은
옥빛 살짝 나는 색.

중력을 거부한
먼지가 언니의
창백한 손가락
사이로

흐르기 때문에.

Tattoo

In deep serenity
When small beings were engraving landscapes
In the dim air,

You were embedded in my whole body
As you were the masterpiece of the unknown artists

Onto my whole body
A transparent shadow fell

At the heartbeat accelerated
My forehead and lips were dipped by the shadow
And in a breathtaking moment
My ankles and toenails were stained by it, too

I trace the shadow with my bare hands
And I, at times, became your shadow, too
My whole body turning into your tattoo
Was a miracle, an overwhelming one at that

It is a miracle in which I murmur:
Because I have a shadow,
I am alive, I could be alive, I became alive

Into the air
Flied the sound of a dry river
And while a shapeless butterfly flowed

The miracle in thick serenity
Became quiet, and quieter,
Then it finally folded its wings
To land

To land on my whole body in transparency.

타투

짙은 고요 속
미물들이 어슴푸레 허공에
풍경화를 새기는 동안

뜨거운 잉크로 온몸에 배어들었다, 당신은
무명의 화가들이 수놓은 열심의 작품

나의 온몸 위로

투명한 그림자가 쏟아진다

빨라진 심박에
미간도 입술도 그림자에 젖고
숨 막히는 호흡에
발목도 발톱도 그림자에 물들고

맨손으로 그림자를 더듬는다
당신의 그림자가 되어도 본다
온몸이 당신의 타투로 변하는 이것은
기적, 분명히 너무한 기적

그림자가 있으니 나는
살아있다, 살아졌다, 살아났다,
중얼거리는 기적

허공으로
메마른 물소리가 날고
형체 없는 나비가 흐르는 동안

짙은 고요 속 기적이
조용해지다가, 더 조용해지다가
날개를 접는다,
내려앉는다

나의 온몸 위로 투명히 내려앉는다.

Sense of Belonging

When you can self-love
Even when they disapprove
I feel so proud that
I am your woman

Your insistence on our
Keeping an adequate distance
Always reminds me that
I am a person of my own.

소유

모든 이가 당신이 틀렸다 할 때
자신을 사랑할 수 있는 당신을 보면
내가 당신의 여자인 게
자랑스럽습니다

우리 사이에도 적당한
거리를 지켜 달라 이야기하는
당신을 보면 나는 온전히
나의 사람인 것을 깨닫습니다.

We Cuddled and Laughed at Six Forty-four

We cuddled like a pair of cocoons

Awaiting their metamorphosis

Under the warmth of our lasting familiarity

That was sugar sweet and only sometimes

Bitter or too salty.

Crisp beams of youthful sun shined

On our bronze bodies wearing

No strand of silk

But softer,

Showered with ticklish humor

Unbearable and light

Afraid of bursting we hugged

Each other's laughter

And instead wriggled our toes

Transparency of the morning

Seized us in a coma

Which did not want to

Pop the unconscious bliss

While the sun kept sending us

His altruistic kisses.

우리는 껴안고 웃었다, 여섯 시 사십 사 분에

우리는 나비가 되기 전에 지속하는
설탕같이 달지만, 간혹 쓰거나 짠
친숙함의 따스한 온도 속에
한 쌍의 누에고치처럼 몸을 말았습니다
젊은 햇살이 바스락 구릿빛 몸에 닿았고
비단 한 올 자아내지 못했지만
우리는 더 부드러웠습니다
참을 수 없이 가벼운 농담은 간지러워서
터질까 두려워 서로의 웃음을 껴안고
대신 발가락을 꼼틀거렸습니다
아침의 투명이 우리를 무의식으로 빠뜨리고
반의식조차 벗고 있음을 깨닫지 못할 때
기쁨을 깨고 나오고 싶지 않은 그 시각
해는 계속, 계속, 자애로운 빛을 우리에게 보냈습니다.

Night Ablaze

Treaties unspoken

Hearts pressed

Pumping urges

Air compressed

Passion moist

Hushed fullness

Plump courtesy

Composed neither

Beast unwinding

Shh...

Night ablaze

Sleep, my dear...

타는 밤

무언의 조약
짓눌린 심장
두근대는 충동
압축된 공기
젖은 열정
조용한 가득 참
노골적 예의
나조차 흐트러진
풀어진 짐승
쉿…
밤이 타고 있다
잘 자, 내 사랑….

Junction

At a junction
Our perpendicular lives met

Beautiful distortion
Under spectacular sunset

A near illusion
That sweet atmosphere set

A rare interaction
That's an overparticular act

A mere infatuation
That's a silly vascular fret

A compunction
Was an unfamiliar regret

Yet your contour, a delineation
Of an obscure silhouette.

고차로

수직의 삶이
교차하는 길에

환영같은 일몰이 드리워
왜곡으로 존재하네

교점은 드물어
이변에 가깝고

혈관이 잠시 놀란
장난뿐일지라도

양심의 가책은
흔치 않은 후회였고

너의 옆모습은
음영의 윤곽이네.

Precociousness

Filled with a child's excitement,

There was no longer a child

He was wise enough

To know

He was precocious

No more.

조숙함

소년의 흥분에 휩싸여
소년은 더는 없었다
그는 현명했다
자신이 더는 조숙하지 않음을 알 만큼.

New Hampshire Wind Blew in Seoul

New Hampshire visited me
In his attire formal
In Seoul a day later
Than my birthday years after
I had left him, cold
Holding a hat of clouds
And a bow tie of the spring wind,
The gentleman said:
"If you do not resent me,
Let me visit again
With a bouquet of leaves
Hand-dyed in different hues
Of reds in couple months"
Reminiscent, I could not believe
What a long way he had come.

뉴햄셔의 바람이 서울에 불어왔네

뉴햄셔가 정장을 차려입고
내 생일 며칠 뒤
서울로 나를 찾아왔네
나는 차갑게 그를 떠났건만
구름으로 만든 모자를 손에 들고
봄바람으로 만든 나비넥타이를 하고
신사는 말했다
"나를 미워하지 않는다면
몇 달 뒤에 다시 찾아올게요.
손수 염색한
여러 색조의 붉은
이파리의 부케를 들고요"
기억에 잠겨, 나는
그가 얼마나 먼 길을 왔나,
믿을 수 없었네.

Rooftop

Where it provided us a roof

Where we lay down to listen to the night rain

Where dew fell before anywhere else

Where twilight hit first

Where you could see the sigh

Where light slowly dimmed down

A santuary

For all beautiful beings.

옥상

지붕이 되어 준 곳
함께 누워 밤비를 듣던 곳
이슬이 처음 내리는 곳
노을이 먼저 닿는 곳
한숨이 눈에 보이는 곳
빛이 스러지는 곳

아름다운 것들의
안식처.

Third Color --

Sadness and Anguish

All of your life
As an adult
Is spent for
Healing the wound
You got as a kid.

슬픔과 고통

어른으로 사는 삶은
아이였을 때
입었던 상처를
치유하는 데
전부 사용된다.

Anger

Time when it's so hard to forgive
When you burn just not to curse,

It dies

Whether it be beauty, or poetry,
Or faith, or an organ, that dies,
In silence, in violence,
With defiance, without a bias,

Let them be and let me suffer
And let my poetry brood,

Just for a moment

In silence

In violence

With defiance

Without a bias

Wait until tears

Are

Done

Falling.

화

저주하지 않기 위해
온 힘을 다하느라
용서하지 못할 때가 있다

죽는다

아름다움이, 시가,
믿음이, 신체의 일부가,
죽는다

고요히, 격렬히, 도전하다
편견 없이, 죽는다

그들을 살게, 나를 견디게,
나의 시가 번식하게 하소서

그저 잠시

고요히
격렬히
도전하다
편견 없이

눈물이 흐르기를
다하게
하소서.

Validity

All your feelings were valid
Even when you turned pallid

Vanity in your eyelid
More substantial than solid

Your imagination wicked
At least not faked

Feel free to be twisted
For the sake of the untainted.

근거

모든 감정엔 근거가 있다
네가 창백한 표정을 할 때조차

너의 눈꺼풀 속 허영은 건실하고
무엇보다 진솔하다

너의 상상은 짓궂으나
최소 꾸밈은 없다

마음껏 꼬여라
때 묻지 않도록.

You said life is good as it is full of love
But it is mundane as it is full of tears

Love, love,
tears, tears,

사랑이 있어 좋은 인생이라 하셨죠,
눈물이 많아 그저 평범하네요

사랑, 사랑,
눈물, 눈물,

Despair

Merged underwater

Wanting to feel better

Seeking the altar

Only to further clutter

Minds that alter

And footsteps, falter.

절망

깊은 물 속에 잠겨
행복을 기원하며
신을 찾으나
혼란스러운 마음은
더욱 엉클어지고
걸음마저 헛디디네.

Primal Torture for the Accused of Gluttony
–A Memo at a Jazz Bar

Time was dyed in the color

Of the torturous hopes and I was in the

Want of all things that were not mine

The atmosphere was brightly dark

Like that mini extravagant black dress

That sizzled as it burned on a flame

In the dancing flurry meeting

The starting lovers' eyes

At the jazz bar lively

While rain drizzled outside and

The bassist plucked his gaunt fingers on

Crescendos and decrescendos of his life

Saturated in Black and Blue

Fun to play with, unlikely to yield much,

Igniting the lovers' hearts with the

Craze of one thousand blossoms of evil,

Insatiable quench for the unreachable

Purity of water from underneath the solution

Salty martini, an irrepressible desire

Gasping for the tingle of the air

Lurking behind the most refined gestures

Of tossing champagne glasses,

To have and make their own,

—Maybe even a child—the burning primal

Obsession that was their

Dripping wet gluttony.

탐욕을 벌하는 원시적 고문
-어느 재즈바에서의 메모

시간은 희망으로 고문하고
내 것이 아닌 모든 것은 부족하게 마련이었다
나는 내 것이 아닌 것들이 모자라는 중이었다
에워싼 분위기는 사치스러운 블랙 미니 드레스가
춤의 찬란 속 불꽃에 마냥 타들어 가는 것처럼
화려하게 깜깜했다
시작하는 커플들은 생기 있게 이 재즈바에서
서로의 눈빛을 응시하고 창밖에는 비가 쏟아졌다
그동안 베이시스트는 수척한 손가락으로
블랙 앤 블루에 포화한 자기 인생의
크레센도와 데크레센도를 내내 뜯고 있었다

장난은 재미있게, 남는 것은 별로 없게,
연인들의 가슴을 천 송이 악의 꽃으로
뜯어내고 있었다
술 용액 하부의 닿을 수 없는, 짠 마티니 아래의
물의 순수함을 향한 채울 수 없는 갈증은
샴페인 잔을 부딪히는 가장 우아한 손짓 뒤로
따르는 한 줌 공기를 위한 숨 막힘
서로 가지려 하고 서로의 것으로 만들려 하는
—어쩌면 아이조차—타 들어가는 원시의 집착이자
뚝뚝 떨어지는 젖은 탐욕이었다.

—희망 고문, 서로를 가지려는 탐욕에 대한 벌

Punishment

On some nights upon waking, you wonder:

"Is this a punishment?"
"It may be."

Then you murmur half asleep:

"It must be."

벌

가끔 잠에서 깨어
벌인가,
벌이구나

벌임이 분명하다,
무심코 되뇔 때가 있지.

My God is, My Idol is,

Genius

You picked the precise method
It was eminent
As you did not really pick it

You picked without picking
The pain of not being able to know,
That I know while not knowing, and I cry

You are genius
You are crying, too.

나의 신은 나의 우상은

귀재십니다

정확한 방법을 택하셨나이다
택하신 것이 아니기에
탁월하셨나이다

알 수 없는 고통을
택하지 않은 채 택하시기에
모른 채 압니다, 웁디다

귀재시더이다
당신도 웁디다.

Silent Night,

A night without even one flower.

고요한 밤,
한 떨기 없는 밤.

On the Day when My Heart is Cold

On days when my heart is too cold
I wish I did not have a heart

To you who do not have a heart,
I declare no war

And I let my heart sleep.

마음이 시린 날

마음이 너무 시린 날엔
마음이 없으면 좋으련만

마음이 없는 자여,
경쟁할 마음 없어

마음을 재운다.

Fourth Color --

Parting and Loss

At times, parting,
Two people becoming two again,
Like they initially were,
Is as marvelous as
Two people falling in love,
Getting together
To become like one.

이별과 상실

때론 헤어짐이,
두 사람이 비로소 다시
둘이 되는 일이,
일찍이 둘이 사랑을 시작하며
하나가 되는 과정만큼이나
의미가 있다.

Murky-skyed Morning

Rain hung

Onto

Cloud's bosom

Gravid

Birds sang

For their mistresses

Placid

I sank

Into hopes of your coming

Invalid

Something fell

In this morning

Murky-skyed.

흐린 아침

비는 무겁게
구름의 가슴에
매달렸고

새는 평화롭게
애인을 향해
노래했고

나는 부질없게
네가 올 희망에
잠겼다

흐린 이 아침
무언가
널어졌다.

Spring Night's Forest

Father's dry cough accumulates
to become a spring night's forest
The hours fall off the cliff to become our time

I lived in that forest for 20 years

The forest closed its eyes
and is lying on its bed, still
Spring's forest is heavily walking
towards the period mark

Who put the period there?

The forest only walks forward
that even if I reach my hands backward
They touch nothing, not even the closest darkness

Your short breaths turned into cigarette smoke
And I, to this date, calculate
how much of our time it cut away

In the time that breaths made and breaths took away,
The spring forest
Continues to get dimmer

I hold onto the night with joints that are hardening
And try to walk to where the period is,
Just to where the period is.

봄밤의 숲

아버지의 마른기침이 고여 봄밤의 숲이 되고
절벽의 시간들이 떨어지며 우리의 시간이 되고

그 숲에서 20년을 살았네

눈감은 숲이 병상에 누웠다, 여전히
봄의 숲이 마침표를 향해 뚜벅이며 걷고 있다

누가 마침표를 찍었나

숲은 앞으로만 걸어서 뒤로 손을 뻗어도
잡히는 것이 없어, 가장 가까운 어둠조차

당신의 짧은 숨들은 담배 연기를 게워내고
나는 우리의 시간이 얼마나 깎이는지
셈하여 보곤 해, 여전히

숨이 만들고 숨이 깎은 시간 속
봄의 숲은,
계속 어두워지기만 하네

굳어가는 관절로 잡히지 않는 밤을 잡고
마침표가 있는 곳 딱 거기까지만
걸어가야 해.

The Best Thing I've Ever Done

Having invited the sunshine fully into my eyes
Having let the sunshine flow out of my eyes
Not having stopped my tears to overflow
with the sunshine
Having allowed the silver rain to fall
Not having been ashamed for crying
Having said that I cried, because I cried
When you asked me why I cried,
Having honestly answered,
"Because I'm not used to your warmth"
Having made you embarrassed
However, not having consoled you
Having let you suffer the temperature of my tears
While you were crying and crying,
Not having even asked you why you were crying.

내가 가장 잘한 일

망막으로 햇살을 받아내다
햇살이 넘치도록 내버려 둔 일
햇살과 함께 눈물을 쏟아버린 일
은비가 내리도록 허락한 일
울었다, 라고 말하며 창피하지 않았던 일
울었기 때문에, 울었다고 말한 일
왜 우냐는 당신의 질문에
당신 다정함이 어색해서, 라고 솔직했던 일
당신을 당황하게 만든 일
그러고도 위로하지 않은 일
내 눈물의 온도에 당신이 괴로워하게 둔 일
당신이 펑펑 우는 동안 내버려 둔 일
왜 우냐고 묻지 않은 일.

Empty Space

I become an open quotation mark
And wait for you—you do not come to me
To close me—I,
An open quotation mark without its mate,
am awaiting
In an infinite time
I am waiting while I am not waiting

Some days I become an open parenthesis
And face the beginning of time
In which you do not come for me, awaiting the end
I become a vast, open, parenthesis

I become a space that is
Alone, empty, and without an end.

텅 빈

나는 열리기만 한 따옴표가 되어
너를 기다렸다―너는 닫는 따옴표가 되어
내게 오지 아니한다―나는,
짝을 잃은 따옴표가 되어 무한의 시간을
기다리고 있다
기다리지 않은 채 기다리는 것이다

어떤 날은 열린 괄호가 되어
내게 오지 않는 끝을 기다리는
시간의 시작을 맞는다
광활한 열린 괄호가 되는 것이다

홀로 비어 있는, 닫힘 없는,
그런 공간이 되는 것이다.

Untitled

One says it is dawn
One says it is dusk

One says he cries a river as he is sad
One says she cannot cry as she is too sad

One says it went too quickly as it was 1/8 of his life
One says it was too long as it was 1/6 of her life

The meaningless relativity
That is mere difference in degree.

제목 없음

누구는 아침 놀이라 하고
누구는 저녁 놀이라 하고

누구는 슬프니 강만큼 운다 하고
누구는 슬퍼서 눈물도 안 나온다 하고

누구는 자기 인생의 1/8이여 후딱 갔다 하고
누구는 1/6이여 아깝다 하고

정도의 차이여서
의미 없는 상대성.

Fifth Color --

Back to Nature

Do some rivers become poems in one's memory?

다시 자연으로

어떤 강은 기억 속 시가 되는 건가….

A River Whose Name You Won't Remember

And one day
You will meet a river
Whose name you cannot remember

However,
You will cross that river
in your sleep constantly

As you cross it,
You will feel with your fingertips
An unmemorable old man's

Wrinkles that are its ruffles
You will stand in it like a knar
Of a tree owned by a stranger.

이름 없는 강

그러던 어느 날은
이름을 기억할 수 없는
강줄기도 만날 것이다

그러나,
그 강을 당신은 늘
꿈결 속에 건널 것이다

건너면서 손끝으로
기억할 수 없는
한 노인의 주름살 같은

강의 물결을 느낄 것이다
어떤 이가 소유한 나무의
옹이 마냥 그 강 속에 서리라.

The Red Morning

In the morning in which I am suffering from serenity
A young oak is playing the wind

In red,
We cannot disappear into the sunshine

Every moment that we disappear,
the sunshine is too red,
That we are simply listening to the wind

Whenever the fragile leaves turn in the air
A baby cries in some household
Sparrows and pebbles are filling in the gap
Of notes that the baby skips as he cries

A morning like a twilight is passing by
In red,

While the height of the oak is growing

just a little bit

We write letters to each other

Facing each other, missing each other's voices,

In the morning in which I suffer from serenity,

Morning in which I disappear while suffering,

Morning in which I take everything inside,

While the oak's height is growing just a little bit,

We disappear into a dream where there are many trees

But we end up having dreams of being born

In red,

We are coming into the world.

붉은 아침

평온에 시달리는 아침
어린 떡갈나무가 바람을 연주하고 있다

빨갛게,
햇살 속으로 우리는 사라질 순 없다

사라지는 순간순간 햇살이 빨개서
우리는 바람을 듣고 있다

여린 나뭇잎 공중에서 뒤집힐 때마다
어느 집 아이가 운다, 울다가
서툴게 빼먹은 음표들을
참새와 돌멩이들이 채우고 있다

노을 같은 아침이 지나가고 있다
빨갛게,

떡갈나무의 키가 아주 조금 자라는 동안
우리는 서로에게 편지를 쓴다
얼굴을 맞대고 서로의 목소리가 그리워

평온에 시달리는 아침
시달리다 사라지는 아침
내 안으로 모두 다 삼키는 아침

떡갈나무의 키가 아주 조금 자라는 동안
나무가 나오는 꿈속으로 사라지다가,

태어나는 꿈을 꾸고야 만다

빨갛게,
우리는 태어나고 있다.

Mermaid

It was raining

Under your roof

With worn-out wallpapers

According to the weather forecast

The humidity would prolong

So much that a mermaid could live

Reason your organs were wet

Was because you could not flood

It was because monsoon only came to your inside

Even though weather forecast said

A mermaid could live,

They said this year's monsoon was a dry one

You did not like that saying

What good is it if a monsoon is dry?

You quietly dropped your head

You, more fragile than I thought,

Were hurt by my quiet words that day

And under your roof, onto your bed,

Rain was sweeping in

In more number of colors

Than our eyes could detect

That day, you flooded

Somebody cried, somebody was hurt,

Somebody was wet, and somebody kept getting dry.

인어

비가 오고 있었다
당신의 지붕 아래로
낡은 벽지와 함께 흐르고 있었다
일기예보에 따르면
인어가 살 수도 있겠다 싶을 만큼
습한 날씨가 지속되고 있다고 했다
장기까지 축축하게 젖었던 것은
범람하지 못했기 때문이었다
당신의 안으로만 장마가 왔기 때문이었다
일기예보에 따르면
인어가 살 수도 있겠지만
올해의 장마는 마른장마라고 했다
당신은 그 말을 싫어했다
장마가 말랐으면 무슨 소용이람
조용히 고개를 떨구던 당신

생각보다 더 여렸던 당신이
내 조용한 말들에 상처받은 날
당신의 지붕 아래로, 당신의 침상 위로
우리가 볼 수 있는 색보다
더 여럿의 색을 입은 비가 들이쳤다
당신이 범람하던 그 날
누군가는 울었고 누군가는 아팠고
누군가는 젖었고 누군가는 말라갔던.

I Remember a Tree who Held So Many Secrets

The tree warped
Holding so many secrets
That lurked

When I remarked
"What toil you must have endured,"
Tree's heart barked

Sparkling tales were uncorked
As his branches sparked
While his poetry worked

Ears perked
The Earth turned, a minute arced*
To listen to a tree's tale

*A minute of arc is 1/60 of a degree.

너무 많은 비밀을 듣고 서 있던 나무를 나는 기억한다

나무가 뒤틀렸다
요동치는 비밀을
너무 많이 간직하느라

대체 어떤 고통을 견뎠나?
내가 혼잣말로 이야기하자,
나무의 심장이 짖었다

반짝이는 이야기를 따는 동안
나무의 시가 말이 되었고
가지가 불탔다

귀를 쫑긋 세우고
나무의 이야기를 들으려
지구는 굴절된 작은 각도를 돌았다.

At a Spring Beach Where
There was the Aspiring White Sand

Soapy white waves were rubbing the sand

With its breaking away bubbles

That were so much rougher than

Their petit lacy looks

The sound of ebbs and tides

Endlessly caressed the cerebrum

That ordered hearts not to skip a beat

At the extraordinary theory

That the seascape was lecturing

The strangely deep silence was

Probably imaginary

but it really deafened

The cacophony of lyrics

Chanted in ordinary routines

Of daily lives.

큰 포부를 가진 하얀 모래가 있는 봄의 바다에서

비누처럼 하얀 파도는
부서지는 물방울로 모래를 쓸고 있었고
모래는 작은 레이스 같은 외관보단 훨씬 단단했다
바다의 겹치는 비범한 이론을 강의 중이었고
대뇌는 끊임없이 심장에 박자를 놓치지 않기를 당부했다
이상할 만큼 깊은 침묵은 상상이었겠지만
일상의 가사가 만든 불협화음은 정말로 잠재워 지고 있었다.

I am a Dew

There is no room for a dew
When it is raining

The entirety wears a murky hue
Without a silver lining

What fall are too blue
For me to stand, shining

Please come for my rescue
Important is your timing

When you come—

Please bring me some tea to brew
And a hope for the sun rising

Well then—

Without further ado
My lips I shall be biting.

나는 이슬이에요

하늘이 울면
이슬은 갈 곳을 잃고
은빛 테두리 없는
진흙의 색조를 입어요.

빛나며 견디기엔
떨어지는 것들이 너무 파래서
제발 나를 구하러 와요,
알맞은 시각에요.

오실 적에—

끓일 차와 해가 뜰 거란
희망 좀 가져다주세요

제발 작별하지 않겠다는
약속도 지켜 주세요.

저, 그럼—

더는 말없이
침묵을 지키죠.

Flower

My flower tells me:

You shall leave me alone

So I can live on my own

That will be the way I will be loved greatly

Only, do not stop sending me your warm gaze.

꽃

나의 꽃이 말한다
너는 내버려 두라
스스로 살게 내버려 두라
내가 크게 사랑받을 방법이다

따스한 눈길만은 멈추지 말아다오.

The Birth of a Grandmother
(A Night-time Tale 2)

Her forehead was deeply contemplating
Upon waking. The girl was feverish
From her numerous ages.
Her joints were deterred from
Standing up too quickly but her being
Had grown light enough. And her complexion
Was richer in other things, only lacking
In illuminants.
The root of her problems, though
Lay in the tale that was her great grandmother's
Endowment which in turn, she inherited
After yesterday's daybreak that was
Stored in the household's
Archive for ever more,
Inflicting un-forgetfulness ever after.

What a curse, indeed, those dusts on
The windowpane are white as a scallion's
Roots in hundreds of strands and yet,
Her first speech came very gently when
She uttered,

"Mm,"
Later that night.

할머니의 탄생
(옛날이야기 2)

일어나면서부터 이마는 깊은 생각에 잠겨
소녀는 수없는 나이로 뜨거웠지.
관절이 너무 빨리 서는 것을 막았지만
존재는 다행히 가벼워 져 있었어.
피부는 다른 것으로 풍부했고
빛을 내는 것들만 잃었을 뿐이었지.
문제의 근원은 그러나,
증조할머니가 남기신 기억의 서재였어.
기억이란 정말…
그 후 영원히 오래오래 잊지 못하는 것이었지.

창틀의 먼지가 정말 하얗지 않니?
백 갈래 파 뿌리처럼 말이야….

할머니는 그러고는 저녁이 돼서야
부드럽게 그 날의 첫 마디를 뱉으셨다.

"음"

Phenomena Relevant

Pouring dawn comes unforced
Like rain that falls unannounced

After a steamy night
Following a scalding day

Fate comes unforeseen:
Birth drags lazily loitering

Death is quick

A thought is consequential
Like action turning into a habit

The unforeseen
That were predictable.

연관

새벽에 비가 세차게 왔다.
아무도 강요하지 않았는데 왔다

열기의 밤 뒤 증기의 낮 후
소식 없이 왔다

보이지 않는 곳으로부터 왔다.
느리게 배회하는, 게으른,
긴 탄생 뒤에 오는

죽음은 잠깐

상념은 결과를 가져왔다
몸짓이 습관이 되듯,

보이지 않는 것들은
퍽
예측할 수 있게 왔다.

Golden Willow

Golden willow
Dips her fingers
To thaw November river

Inky stars
Spread through
Deep down the river.

금빛 버드나무

금빛 버드나무
11월의 강을 녹이며
손가락을 담근다

별빛 잉크가
강 구석구석 퍼지며
깊숙이 물들이네.

In the City with my Cat

Oh, my sweety,

A ball of purity

So itty-bitty

You're full of vanity

Our mutuality

Keeps my sanity

In New York City

That would've been empty

Without my Kitty.

도시에서 고양이와

아, 나의 고양이,
순수한 털 뭉치
너무 작고 귀여워
너는 허영 가득해
우리가 함께하기에
나는 오늘도 제정신이야.
뉴욕이란 도시는
나의 고양이 없이는
텅 비어 있었을 거야.

Picnic

I lived a day too long
In a moment of one breath
Humming and whistling
As if on a picnic

With a bunch of friends
On a yellow school bus
Wearing red, blue, stripes
And polka dots
On a spring day

A festivity thrown
By the mellow sky
For angelic minds
Of innocuous people
Brave and forever young

Running and tumbling
We did not even notice
How tired we grew
It was a day quite long
Indeed, gone too quickly.

소풍

너무 긴 하루를
한 숨의 찰나에 보냈다
소풍 날
흥얼거리며, 휘파람 불듯

노랑 스쿨버스에 한가득 타고
빨강, 파랑, 줄무늬,
그리고 땡땡이 옷을 입은 친구들과
봄소풍 가듯

용감하고 영원히 젊은
무해한 사람들의
천사 같은 마음에
부드러운 하늘이
잔치를 벌인 날처럼

뛰고 구르다 보니
피곤한 줄을 몰랐네
꽤나 긴 하루가
정말 빨리 기고 있다.

Life

Father had said that it was
A sea of hardships.
Mother had said it was
As simple as an egg.

The child laughed,
Picturing an egg
Swimming in the ocean.

That ocean was so broad
And the egg, which was I,
Had such a thin shell

That I laugh,
Wondering how
I still didn't break.

삶은

아버지는 고해의 바다라 하시고
어머니는 달걀이라 부르셔
삶은 달걀의 헤엄인가,
아이는 웃었다.

그 바다는 넓었고
나란 달걀은 작았고
내 껍데기는 너무 여려
어찌 아직 안 깨졌나,
웃는다.

1

ISBN 979-11-89129-78-1